THE ULTIMATE HOUSEHOLD HANDBOOK

Household tips that really work

Maxwell Stein

The Ultimate Household Handbook
Maxwell Stein

Copyright © MMVII de Swartes Ltd, London

Published MMVII by The Windsor Group,
The Old School House, 1 St John's Court,
Moulsham Street, Chelmsford,
Essex CM2 0JD

Copyright © MMVII The Windsor Group (This Edition)

Typeset by SJ Design and Publishing, Bromley, Kent

ISBN 1-903904-23-4

Contents

Notice To Readers

Although every effort has been made to ensure the accuracy of the information provided in this publication, neither the author nor the publishers can accept responsibility or liability for that information, this including any of the opinions or advice expressed in the following pages.

Introduction

Most of us have been given good tips in our time, and there are some we have used. But, if you are honest with yourself, they have been mostly ignored, which means that many good ideas are lost.

I started my collection of tips many years ago at a time when I was deeply interested in how things were made. I found that people who indulged in the arts and crafts, all had their special short cuts to achieve the end result. Then there are the professionals and tradesmen; each and every one has there own idea on how to go about doing their work.

It is amazing to see how easily the saddler repairs a saddle or piece of harness. It is fascinating to watch a furniture restorer make old or damaged pieces look like new. But neither of these artisans would be able to do their craft without the little tricks and shortcuts that have been handed down by generations before them. Would you think of never washing a frying pan after use? Top chefs would never dream of letting the 'washer-up' wash their frying pans; rather they scour them with salt and oil to keep them in good condition. Did you ever collect stamps when you were young, and wonder how to remove stamps from envelopes successfully? All you have to do is place the envelope in the freezer for a few hours. You'll then be able to easily lift the stamps off with a pair of tweezers.

Such tips are often simple and easy to use and I have gathered many over the years. Great tips make light of difficult tasks, they make objects round the home last longer, and look better. So, it seemed the obvious thing to do was to collate as many of these tips as possible and to publish them for all to read. Some of them may seem odd or old fashioned, but, they have worked for others, and hopefully they will work for you. Many readers will see a good tip and be able to improve on it . . . that is what we call progress. Hopefully if that is the case, the reader will make a note of it and pass it on so that others can benefit.

Section 1

Your Home

CHROME FIXTURES

- ❑ Use new or used fabric softener sheets to shine the chrome-plated fixtures in your bathroom and kitchen. The chrome will sparkle like new!
- ❑ Your chrome fixtures will come up like new when you clean them with lemon juice. Just rub them with the pulp of half a lemon after you have used the juice for drinks or for cooking.
- ❑ Use rubbing alcohol on a cleaning cloth to remove soapy scum from chrome-plated fixtures.
- ❑ To remove rust from chrome, rub the affected area with aluminium foil.

SHOWER CURTAINS

Shower curtains quickly become stained with mildew spots if you don't clean them regularly. Use a solution of warm soapy water containing 20% chlorine bleach when washing your shower curtains to keep the mildew spots at bay.

BATHMATS

Bathmats will quickly become grubby and smelly if left in the bath. Always hang them on a rail to dry when not in use.

BATHS

- Prevent a messy tidemark in the bath by adding a little bubble bath or washing-up liquid to the bathwater.
- Clean behind bath and sink taps and reach other awkward spots with an old toothbrush dipped in disinfectant.
- Old net curtains make excellent bath cleaners as they are mildly abrasive and do not scratch.

BREADBINS

Stop mildew forming by regularly wiping out the breadbin with a clean cloth dabbed in a solution of vinegar and water. Two tablespoons of vinegar to 450ml of water is sufficient.

GROUT CLEANER

Use hydrogen peroxide to get rid of the hard-to-remove mildew that collects in the grouting around the bathroom taps. Pour it on directly and it instantly softens the dirt so you can remove it with just one wipe! It will also whiten the grout!

STAINED TOILET BOWLS

Coke is a cheap alternative to expensive toilet cleaners. When you have a bottle of coke or Pepsi that has gone flat, pour it down the loo last thing at night. By morning you will have a shiny clean bowl. Coke is supposed to dissolve limescale as well.

TILE CLEANER

❑ For economical as well as sparkling results, there's no need to replace worn-out old bathroom tiles. Try the acid test and see for yourself by sprinkling a little boric acid on the tiles before washing.

❑ When you run out of your regular bathroom cleaner, use hot soapy water with a drop of ammonia in it. You'll find that it's great for cutting through greasy bathroom marks.

CLEANING WINDOWS

❑ Add a few tablespoonfuls of white vinegar to your water when cleaning windows, and watch them come up shining every time.

❑ If you haven't got a chamois leather to polish your windows, use newspaper; it works just as well.

GUM REMOVER

❑ To remove sticky gum residue from plastics and bottles, just spray a little WD40 on the gum and leave it for a few minutes. Clean off the WD40 with soapy water.

❑ White spirit will remove gum residue from glass and hard plastics.

VASE CLEANER

To remove a dried on water mark from the bottom of a glass vase, just fill with water to just above the mark and add two Alka-Seltzer tablets. Leave for 24 hours for the tablets to work.

SILVER POLISH

Baking soda smoothed on with a damp cloth is a great way to clean silver. Afterwards rinse and let the items stand to dry.

METAL POLISH

For a great metal polish, use blackboard chalk rubbed onto the metal with a clean cloth. Polish off the residue with another clean cloth.

MIRRORS

Polish mirrors with cold tea rather than commercial cleaners. Or try polishing glass and mirrors with a screwed-up piece of newspaper.

DECANTERS

- ❑ To clean out decanters, fill with a solution of warm water and vinegar in equal parts mixed with half a cupful of clean sand. Shake hard and leave to stand.
- ❑ If the stopper gets stuck in a decanter, apply a few drops of warmed cooking oil around the edge. Leave in a warm place for half an hour or so, then gently tap the stopper with a wooden spoon handle.

EARTHENWARE CLEANER

Clean unglazed earthenware with a solution of hot water and vinegar or salt.

WOODEN FLOORS

When cleaning wooden floors, fill a spray bottle with one part vinegar to three parts water. Spray the solution on the floor and use a sponge mop to clean.

MARBLE

Stained marble can be cleaned by lightly scouring with finely powdered borax, and then washing with warm water applied with a cloth.

STONE

Stone, particularly if porous, is liable to retain stains of any kind, and if washing with strong soda is not sufficient, fuller's earth should be tried.

CHINTZ FABRIC

❑ Chintz curtain and coverings that have become soiled through everyday wear and tear can be cleaned without washing the fabric. Shake or brush the materials, then rub with a clean, damp cloth, and finish by rubbing dry breadcrumbs well into the fabric and brushing with a clean, stiff brush.

❑ Dark coloured chintz can be dry cleaned by applying hot dry bran and ammonia crystals. Put the fabric into a large bowl or tub with a cupful of hot dry bran, add a teaspoonful of ammonia crystals, cover the receptacle, and shake vigorously for some minutes. Remove the fabric, shake and brush or vacuum thoroughly, and hang in a current of air for half an hour.

LACE

An excellent way of cleaning real lace is to steep it in milk for several hours, then lightly squeeze. If it is still soiled, rinse in fresh milk, and lightly squeeze again. Hang it out to get partly dry, pulling it out to its shape very carefully. Finally place the lace between two pieces of old soft sheeting and press with a warm iron. This method will be found to give it the old lace colour and appearance.

BROKEN GLASS

Picking up bits of broken glass can be a painful experience if the jagged edges get under the skin. By using your loaf you can make this an easy chore.

Take a slice of dry bread, kneed it into a ball in the palm of your hand, and then press the fragments of broken glass into the ball. Be careful when disposing of the ball of bread: you don't want scavenging animals hurting themselves by trying to eat it.

CANDLE MAGIC

Use these tips to save money, and prevent stains and waxy drips from candles.

❑ The reason why cheap candles are cheap is that they have lots of additives in them, causing them to stain when dripped on surfaces. Only buy candles that have been made with paraffin wax, colour, and stearic acid. The acid helps the candle wax burn away so there is little or no dripping. Beeswax and bayberry wax are occasionally employed as additives, and some candles are scented.

❑ When burning candles, make sure they are placed out of a draught and are not near open windows, fans, or heater vents. Even the best dripless candles will drip if there is a draught near them.

❑ Most candlewax spillages occur because the candlestick is too small. When buying candlesticks make sure that they are big enough to collect any overspills.

❑ Candles should be extinguished with a snuffer. If you don't have one a ceramic egg cup or similar placed over the flame will work equally well. Blowing out the flame can cause the melted wax to dribble down the side of the candle.

❑ To make your candles last longer, don't move them until the wax has solidified.

❑ To remove candlewax from wood, soften the wax with a hair dryer, then remove the wax with a paper towel and wash with a solution of vinegar and water.

❑ To clean a candlestick, place it in the deep-freeze for an hour. The wax will be partially frozen and will chip off more easily.

❑ To get hours more use out of your candles, place them in the deep-freeze compartment for a few hours before use.

CARPET SHOCKS

Wall-to-wall manmade fibre carpets are notorious for building-up static electricity. To stop the static giving you a shock every time you enter the room, lightly spray the carpet with a mixture of one part liquid fabric softener and five parts water.

CARPET BURNS

Treat slight burns on carpets caused by sparks from open fires by rubbing the affected area briskly with the cut surface of a raw onion.

CLOGGED DRAIN

If your drain is clogged with grease, pour one cup of salt and one cup of bicarbonate of soda into the drain followed by a kettle of boiling water. This should do the trick!

DRAUGHTY CHIMNEYS

If you have an older house you can save money on your heating bills by blocking up unused chimneys with plastic foam.

ELECTRIC PLUGS

Put an end to hard-to-pull-out electric plugs in seconds by drawing on the power.

If an electric plug fits too tightly and is difficult to pull out, rub its prongs with a soft lead pencil. Make sure that it is fully removed from the mains when you do so.

FLUORESCENT TUBE PROTECTION

The ends of fluorescent tubes are extremely vulnerable from knocks and bangs when taken down for cleaning, or kept in a cupboard as a spare. You can protect them by putting an old sock over each end. Alternatively, roll the tube in a sheet of corrugated cardboard, then hold the cardboard in place with a sock at each end.

FLUFFY PILLOWS

Rest better, sleep better, by bringing back the fluffiness in your pillows. All you have to do is place them in the tumble dryer. The warm air will work wonders in just a few minutes.

LINOLEUM FLOORS

Make your linoleum look as good as new when you treat your floor to a regular check-up with these super ideas.

❑ To remove scuffs and stains from linoleum, spray with any ordinary hairspray and then wipe it off with a damp cloth.
❑ Hide scratches or burn marks on linoleum floors by painting them with car touch-up paint. The paint will last for ages, and it can be done over and over again.

PACKING CROCKERY

When packing your crockery for transit, reduce the chances of breakage by dipping each piece of crockery in a pan of cold water, then wrapping it in clean paper while it's still wet.

PATIO SLIDING DOORS

When cleaning patio door runners, use a silicone based furniture polish. It will make the doors slide easier as well as cleaning the runners.

PILLOW REFRESHER

Feather pillows can be refreshed in a large capacity washing machine and come out again looking and feeling like new. Place the pillow in its case, into the washer and wash on a warm water, gentle cycle. When finished, run the spin cycle twice to squeeze out most of the water. Tumble dry on gentle cycle, shaking the pillow every ten minutes to prevent the feathers from sticking together.

PREVENT GLASSES FROM CRACKING

Glasses are prone to cracking when boiling water is poured into them. However, by placing a teaspoon in the glass you will prevent this happening. A word of warning though: don't try this with your best glasses, as the composition of old or high quality glass varies a lot, and this can make it unexpectedly vulnerable.

REFRESHING A CARPET OR RUG

Extending the life of your carpets will save you pounds as well as adding colour to your life. You'll also be surprised how much can be done to revive the appearance of worn patches.

- When a carpet or rug begins to look stringy where the treading is heaviest, go down on your hands and knees with some bottles of coloured ink – red, green, blue, etc, and for black use Indian ink. Then paint over the fading pattern with a suitable colour.
- A piece of damp foam rubber will help to remove dog and cat hairs from carpets and upholstery.

SQUEAKY FLOORBOARDS

If your house suffers from squeaky floorboards they can be made quieter by using ordinary talcum powder. Use the type that is unscented, unless of course you want the scent to permeate throughout the house.

SUPER WALLPAPER IDEAS

Expensive wallpapers will last longer and look better if you follow a few home tips from the experts.

- Use this tasty breakfast cereal for cleaning soiled wallpaper. A good deal can be done to freshen wallpaper by gently wiping the walls over with a clean folded duster dipped in a bowl of dry breakfast oat-bran. The bran should be renewed constantly, since it has a tendency for the particles to fall to the floor as the cleaning proceeds.

Before using this technique, brush away the dust from the paper using a soft brush.

□ Oat bran is a splendid reviver, but it will not take away finger-marks that are very dirty. They can be removed by using a piece of India-rubber or, in extreme cases, ink-eraser.

□ Grease marks may be removed by putting two or three thicknesses of blotting-paper in contact with the spot and pressing with a warm iron. The blotting-paper should be changed constantly.

□ To remove dried water-based paint from wallpaper, rub gently with rubbing alcohol. It depends on the quality of the wallpaper dye as to whether some dye will fade when removing paint with this method.

□ Toothpaste is good for removing stains on wallpaper, as it acts as a mild abrasive.

□ If the wallpaper has a small hole in it, use a patch of wallpaper similar in size and design to the place you wish to patch. Tear the paper rather than cutting the paper to size, as this will make the join much less noticeable.

□ When papering over old wallpaper, use a clear lacquer varnish over any greasy spots to stop them coming through to the new paper.

□ Use this smart tip for removing coloured crayon marks on your wallpaper. Warm the crayoning with your hair-dryer, then simply wipe of the marks.

SEWING TOUGH MATERIALS

An old saddler's trick will take the effort out of sewing thick materials. To help the needle penetrate the material, first rub the material with an old candle. This technique is also used for sewing thick carpeting.

GRAMOPHONE RECORDS

Gramophone records can be cleaned with a simple solution of lukewarm water and detergent mixed in a washing up bowl or in the bath. Swirl the record around a few times and pat dry with a paper kitchen towel.

VENETIAN BLINDS

For a quick easy clean for Venetian blinds, wear an old pair of fabric gloves, dip your fingers into warm soapy water, and draw each slat between the fingers. Clean the gloves after every few slats.

VELVET CURTAINS STEAM BATH

Velvet curtains can be made to look as good as new by brushing them well before hanging in a steamy bathroom for an hour or so. Afterwards, let the curtains hang to dry in a warm area away from direct sunlight.

PIANO KEYS

Ensure piano keys stay clean and white by keeping the lid open at all times. Ivory turns dark and yellows if exposed to darkness for long periods.

BROKEN KEYS

Remove a broken key from a lock by dabbing a spot of super glue on the broken off piece. Hold this in position for a while against the piece still in the lock. After a few minutes you should be able to pull out the key as normal.

ADDRESS BOOK

Instead of scribbling alterations into address and telephone books, keep a few self-adhesive labels handy and cut these into tiny strips to cover the affected parts and make way for a tidier amendment.

ADHESIVE TAPE

A small button stuck to the end of a roll of adhesive tape will make the end easier to find.

HEATING THE HOME

A great deal of heat escapes through the walls and cracks in window frames and doors. But ordinary items found in the home can halve your heating bills and keep you warm all winter long, with just a little thought.

- Have your hot water heater lagged or wrap a blanket type insulation around it.
- Use draught excluders. These can be made very inexpensively from tubes of material, sewn at one end, stuffed with old tights or stockings and the gap sewn closed.

❑ Keep the doors of pantries, cabinets and closets closed to avoid valuable heat escaping into them.

❑ During colder weather, wear several layers of loose, warm clothing.

❑ Have your heating checked periodically to make sure it is operating at peak efficiency.

❑ Dust impedes the flow of heat, so clean your radiator surfaces often.

❑ Install your water heater in a place where it will be least exposed to cold weather. Cold weather causes the heater to work harder and costs more in electricity bills.

❑ Use water from the cold tap to do as many household tasks as possible.

❑ Buy logs and heating wood when it is cheapest, during the spring and summer months.

❑ Paste aluminium foil to the wall behind radiators. This will reflect the heat back into the room, which would ordinarily escape through the walls.

❑ In winter, drafts and heat loss can be prevented by hanging thick drapes in front of patio windows and doors. Vertical blinds that have been used in the summer can be left in place behind the drapes as an added draft excluder.

Section 2

Stain Removers

Pet stains, wine stains, beer stains: you name it, someone wants to remove it! Try some of these brilliant ideas, and as long as you throw decorum to the winds and act fast enough, most stains will come out. Whatever you do though, put a clean white pad under the stain and keep renewing it as the stain fades. If the stain is right through the material, work with the wrong side uppermost. Then gently dab the stain with a clean cotton cloth.

Some fabrics should never be treated at home and should be left to the professionals to clean. Among the most common fabrics to be avoided are: velvet, brocade, silk, taffeta and lurex.

AGE STAINS

❑ Old tablecloths and doilies handed down from mother to daughter have happy memories of past times. But they can bear stains from long storage. Spruce them up by dabbing the stains with a mixture of fresh lemon juice and a sprinkling of salt rubbed on the spots. Then give them a gentle wash by hand, followed by a good rinse.

❏ Alternatively, drop an ordinary soluble aspirin in the wash with your whites; it will keep them from getting dingy.

❏ Finally, if you add white vinegar to white clothes that have become yellow, it will turn them white again.

BEER STAINS

Bring the spring back to woollens that have been stained with beer by hand-washing in a mixture of lukewarm water and salt. Afterwards, wash in the normal way.

BEETROOT STAINS

Rub washing-up liquid into the stain with the tips of your fingers, and then apply a few drops of ammonia on a clean cotton cloth. Keep dabbing the stain with the ammonia until it loosens. Afterwards, rinse in lukewarm water.

BIRD DROPPING STAINS

Allow to dry before scraping off excess. Sponge with a weak vinegar and water solution.

BLOOD STAINS

❏ Fresh blood stains are the easiest to remove. Rinse the garment in cold water until all the blood has dissolved. Afterwards, wash in the normal way.

❏ Dried blood stains are a little more difficult. As a first attempt, treat the stain as above, and if that fails add a few drops of ammonia to the water, which should do the trick.

❑ Another method is to soak the affected material in cold salted water, then wash in the normal way.

CHOCOLATE STAINS

First scrape off any excess chocolate. Make up a solution of 50/50 neat biological washing liquid and glycerine, and then blot with a clean cloth. If any of the stain remains, soak the fabric in neat biological detergent. White fabrics can be dabbed with bleach.

COFFEE, COCOA AND TEA STAINS

For coffee, cocoa and tea stains, soak in detergent or in warm water to which one tablespoon of borax or two tablespoons of household ammonia have been added.

COLLAR STAINS

To remove ring around the collar, try this simple trick: wet the collar with warm water, sprinkle liberally with cream of tartar and rub in well. Launder as usual.

CRYSTAL STAINS

To remove stains from crystal, squeeze the juice from half a lemon, soak a cloth in the juice and simply clean your crystal with it.

FRUIT AND BEETROOT STAINS

Remove fruit and beetroot stains by placing the material in a bowl and pouring boiling water directly onto the stain from a height. This should be done immediately after staining.

GRASS STAINS

❑ Pre-treat grass stains on washable fabrics by sponging them first with warm water then dabbing the soiled area with undiluted rubbing alcohol. Wash the item in the usual way.

❑ Apply a small amount of toothpaste on an old toothbrush. Scrub the stain with the toothpaste, then wash in the normal way. Don't use toothpaste that has a coloured stripe through it, as it might discolour the material.

❑ Combine 3 drops of household ammonia with 1 teaspoonful of 6% hydrogen peroxide. Rub on the stain and rinse with water as soon as the stain disappears.

❑ Remove grass stains with a cloth wetted with white vinegar.

INK STAINS

There are several methods of dealing with ink stains, each one depending on the colour and type of ink.

❑ To remove ordinary, water-based blue ink, spray the stain with ultra-hold hairspray, let it dry, then wash in the normal way. If the stain is still wet, sprinkle salt on it, and then brush it off after a few minutes when it has soaked up some of the ink. You may need to repeat this a few times.

- Fresh ink stains on carpets can be soaked with carbonated water, then blotted off with paper towels. Alternatively, sprinkle salt over the spilt ink, and when it has absorbed the ink brush it off carefully. Afterwards treat the stain with carbonated water.
- Blue ink on cuffs and blouses should be soaked in hot milk until the stain disperses. Then wash as normal.
- Dab Indian ink and red ink stains with washing-up liquid and then sponge away using ammonia on a clean cloth.
- Treat the ink from felt tip pens in the same way as blue, water-based ink.
- Removing ball point pen stains is easy with eau-de-cologne, because it usually consists of alcohol and about 2% to 6% perfume concentrate. It is, of course, the alcohol that dilutes the ink, making it easier to wash out the stain with soap and water.
- For marks from ballpoints and felt tip pens, soak the stain in methylated spirit then wash in the usual way.

LIPSTICK STAINS

Remove lipstick by working in petroleum jelly or glycerine to loosen the stain then wash in the usual way.

NEWSPRINT STAINS

Newsprint stains can be removed by applying methylated spirit with a clean, damp cloth.

NICOTINE STAINS

Apply fresh lemon juice directly to the stains and then scrub the skin with pumice stone. Soften the skin afterwards with a good quality hand cream.

OIL STAINS

The best product to remove salad dressing and other oily stains from clothing (especially articles that contain some polyester, which is notoriously difficult to clean), is hair shampoo. Squeeze a little onto the spot, rub lightly, and wash as usual.

PAINT

If possible, treat the stain immediately. Scrape off excess paint before it has time to dry. Water-based paint can be sponged with clean water to remove most of the paint, and then soak the stain in liquid detergent to finish it off. Don't wait until wash day to wash the article; do it straight away in warm water.

Oil-based paint is a different matter. Scrape off excess paint as before, then sponge with white spirit or turpentine. Wash immediately in warm water. Some oil-based paints will have special instructions on the side of the tin for removing spillages.

PERSPIRATION STAINS

Remove perspiration stains by soaking the affected area in a solution of one part ammonia to three parts of water.

RED WINE STAINS

- ❑ Don't worry if you spill a glass of red wine on your nice new carpet. Simply pour white wine over the spillage and mop it up with a clean cloth. It may require a second application of white wine to completely eradicate the stain.
- ❑ Treat dried-on red wine stains with white wine or soak them for several hours in glycerine before washing them out.
- ❑ Small red wine stains on white materials can be treated with equal parts of 6% hydrogen peroxide and water.
- ❑ Remove wine stains from table linen and clothing by covering the mark with wet salt. Leave for about an hour and wash in the normal way.

RUST STAINS

This remedy works on most materials, but be careful as it may bleach out the colour of the material as well. To remove the stain, rub with lemon juice and salt, then leave it in the sun to dry. Repeat the treatment until the stain has gone. Wash as normal.

SAUCE STAINS

Scrape off the excess sauce. Then pre-soak with a mixture of water and liquid washing detergent. Then wash in the normal way.

SHOE POLISH STAINS

Remove shoe polish from clothing by brushing with carbon tetrachloride or rubbing alcohol.

TEA AND COFFEE STAINS

☐ Bring your china up like new with something that you use every day, but never gave it a thought. Ordinary, everyday toothpaste is the ideal cleaner to remove marks on plates caused by the metal cutlery abrading the glazed surface and stains from inside cups. Rub the paste onto the surfaces to be cleaned and leave for a few minutes for it take effect, then wash in the normal way.

☐ Tea and coffee stains on clothing can be removed by soaking the affected area in cold water with a little borax added.

UNDERWEAR STAINS

The subject of stains on unmentionables may be taboo, but someone has to deal with them. Treat the stains with neat liquid detergent before putting them in the wash. Difficult stains can be treated by soaking the garment in a bowl of lukewarm water to which is added a small amount of bleach and liquid detergent. After rinsing, wash in the normal way.

WAX STAINS ON MATERIALS

☐ To remove wax from material, lay a brown paper bag over and under the area that the wax has adhered to.

Using a hot iron, press the paper so that the wax will melt. The wax can then be scraped off the material.

❑ Cigarette ash rubbed in with a finger will remove wax crayon from any smooth surface.

Section 3

Washing

Here are some tips and hints on how to make washing your clothes simple and effective, and how to avoid washday disasters.

- ❑ Wash clothing in cool and cold water where possible. And always rinse in cold water.
- ❑ Buy clothes that don't need dry cleaning and don't have to be ironed.
- ❑ Keep the panel in your tumble drier free from fluff. This helps the air get through and saves on electricity.
- ❑ Stop nylon yellowing by adding some baking soda to the water you use to wash and rinse in.
- ❑ Be careful how much fabric conditioner you use. Too little will be ineffective, too much will make your clothes greasy.
- ❑ Sort your washing into matching loads according to what it says on the care labels. Wash as appropriate and avoid the embarrassment and frustration of 'coloured' whites and streaky coloureds.
- ❑ Always mend tears and holes before washing to prevent the washing action increasing the problem.

- ❑ Close all zips, Velcro and button fastenings. If left open, they might damage other things they come into contact with.
- ❑ Check pockets for pens, paper tissues and money. Pens will cause bad staining and paper tissues become heavily fragmented and almost impossible to remove after the wash.
- ❑ Wash tiny articles like underwear in a pillowcase tied at the open end. This stops them getting lost and prevents them becoming tangled with larger items.
- ❑ For hand washing, dissolve powder properly in hot water and add the solution to hand hot water to work with before submerging items to be washed.
- ❑ When soaking, immerse the whole item in case there is a slight colour change. A plate turned upside down on top of clothes soaking in a bucket will do the trick.
- ❑ Squeeze soapy water through a woollen garment during washing. Don't rub or you will damage the fabric and distort the shape of the garment.
- ❑ Wash silk carefully by hand and iron on the wrong side when still damp, except for wild or tussore silk which is usually ironed when dry.
- ❑ Do not leave damp clothing of different colours in the same basket. The colours can still mix even where items are only slightly damp.
- ❑ When washing new towels, always add a tablespoonful of salt to the water. The salt will set the colour so the towels won't fade as quickly.

- After visiting the pool for a swim, rinse swimsuits and trunks in fresh water to remove the chlorine before washing. Remember, chlorine acts as a bleach on colours, and rots the stitching, so don't leave it too long before washing.
- When washing cotton or woollen sweaters, don't hang them on the line to dry as they will lose their shape. Better to hang them on a plastic coathanger.
- White woollen sweaters should never be hung out in bright sunshine to dry. The hot sun will discolour the wool, making it look yellow and old.
- Wash corduroy trousers inside out. This will help to retain the plush raised look of the wales (the ridges on the cloth).

Section 4

In The Kitchen

CAST IRON PANS

Cast iron pans that have been used for years usually become encrusted with burnt-on fat and food. Usually it's a dirty task to get them clean, so why not try this new cleaner that is said to make cleaning a breeze.

Make-up a paste using cream-of-tarter and white vinegar. Then rub the paste in with a scourer, leave for a while, then wash in hot soapy water.

COFFEE POT CLEAN

The best way to clean a stained coffee pot is to put bicarbonate of soda with a little boiling water in the pot. Bring the pot back to the boil and leave until the coffee stains dissolve. Rinse with hot water when clean.

MICROWAVE CLEAN

Microwave ovens are ideal for cooking casseroles, but when the recipe contains onions and garlic the smell does tend to linger, and normal cleaning doesn't seem to help. If this is your problem, try dissolving two tablespoons of bicarbonate of soda in one cup of water in a small microwave-safe bowl. Turn the microwave to full heat and let the solution boil for a few minutes until the steam condenses on the walls. Then wipe clean with a damp cloth.

DISHWASHER CLEAN

Your dishwasher will stay squeaky clean and free of hardwater deposits if you rinse it through with vinegar.

Once a month place a cup of white vinegar in the bottom of the empty dishwasher and run it through the wash and rinse cycles. This prevents hard deposits from getting a head start. Don't forget to turn off the dishwasher before it goes through the drying cycle.

DISH CLEAN

Add a tablespoon of bicarbonate of soda to your water with your usual washing-up liquid when washing used dishes from the night before. It will cut through the grease as well as soften your hands.

OVEN CLEAN

❑ Heat the oven for 20 minutes then switch off. Place a bowl of strong household ammonia on the top shelf and a bowl of boiling water on the bottom shelf. Leave overnight and in the morning clean the oven with soap and water.
❑ Or, apply a strong solution of bicarbonate of soda and water to the oven walls and shelving. Heat the oven for

20 minutes and allow to cool. Finish by washing with soap and water.

ODOROUS SPONGES

Cellulose sponges used for cleaning in the kitchen tend to get smelly, and the odour transfers onto your hands when you use the sponge. A quick spray of any fabric odour remover will keep that nasty odour away.

SOAP SAVERS

❑ Press a piece of crumpled silver paper or kitchen foil to the dampened underside of a bar of soap. The soap will last longer and there will be less mess.

❑ Collect small pieces of soap until you have enough to fill a cup or jar. Add a few drops of glycerine and steam in boiling water until the mixture softens. When cool, press into a ball and reshape the mixture to make a new bar.

SLIMY DISH CLOTHS

Slimy dish clothes can be revitalised by boiling in a weak solution of white vinegar and water. Two teaspoonfuls of vinegar to one litre of water is enough.

STAINLESS STEEL CLEANER

❑ Use a crumpled-up newspaper to polish stainless steel sink and kitchen units.

❑ To remove stains from saucepans, try cooking rhubarb or apple peel in them.

IVORY HANDLES

Ivory handles on cutlery will quickly discolour if not cared for properly. Keep them looking just like new by rubbing them with a cut, raw lemon.

FAT CATCHER

Line the bottom of your oven and grill pans with tin foil to catch the drips of fat which might otherwise burn and stain. Do the same under boiling rings.

ONION SMELLS

Rid your kitchen surfaces of onion smells by rubbing bicarbonate of soda over the affected area, including your hands if necessary.

KITCHEN NOTICE BOARD

For a simple but effective kitchen notice board, try sticking an attractive polystyrene tile on the wall. This can be left as it is or covered in felt or other suitable material. A few drawing pins are all you need to keep notes, recipes and reminders in place.

KETTLE MAINTENANCE

❑ Empty the kettle after every boiling to avoid scale building up. Heavily-scaled kettles take longer to boil.
❑ To descale a furred-up kettle, fill with equal quantities of vinegar and water. Boil and leave the kettle untouched overnight. Clean and boil several times using fresh water.

❑ Only boil as much water as you need in your kettle. This saves both water and energy.

WASTE DISPOSAL

❑ Keep the waste disposal unit from becoming odorous by dissolving half a cup of washing soda in a pan of boiling water and pouring it down once a week.
❑ Clear debris from the waste disposal by feeding a number of ice cubes down it.

SCALES

Dust scales first with flour before weighing treacle or other sticky substances. You'll find the contents will flow off more easily.

MIXING BOWLS

To prevent a mixing bowl moving around when using it, first place the bowl on a damp cloth.

REFRIGERATORS AND FREEZERS

Make unpleasant smells a thing of the past. Make your appliance more economical to run, and best of all, make it last longer.

❑ Defrost your refrigerator regularly. The more it ices up, the more electricity needed to run it.
❑ Let food cool before putting it in the refrigerator. It takes more energy to cool warm food and, arguably, food cooled artificially is a major health hazard.

- Only open the doors to your freezer and refrigerator when necessary. Warm air rushing into the appliance is a major cause of wasted energy.
- A hand hairdryer is useful for defrosting a refrigerator or freezer in an emergency.
- Wrap all highly-flavoured foods separately before storing in refrigerator or freezer.
- A selection of pastry rounds stored in the freezer makes it easy to prepare pies in a hurry.
- Keep unpleasant odours at bay by storing an open box of baking soda in the refrigerator at all times.

Section 5

Cooking

- ❏ Save energy by using a microwave oven instead of a conventional oven whenever possible.
- ❏ Thaw frozen food before cooking it. Less energy is needed to cook the food.
- ❏ Use the right size range burner for the pan you are using. If you use a small pan on a large burner, so much extra heat is wasted.
- ❏ Don't boil water in an uncovered pan. Water boils more quickly in a covered pan or kettle. And it's safer!
- ❏ Use as little water as possible to cook food.
- ❏ Never throw away fat and rinds on bacon. Instead, grill the rinds and add to casseroles and soups, and use the fat for frying bread and eggs.
- ❏ Use the oven to capacity whenever you have it on for any length of time and always cook in bulk.
- ❏ Stale loaves can be revived by quickly running cold water over them and putting them in a hot oven for ten minutes.
- ❏ Finely chop meat and vegetables for stews. The smaller the pieces, the less time and energy it takes to cook them.

❑ Use a vacuum flask to store soups, stews, even meat and vegetable meals for late arrivals. It's much cheaper and kinder on the food than leaving it in the oven.

❑ Remove cooking odours by boiling a handful of cloves in water for about 30 minutes.

❑ Plan meals and menus using the cheaper varieties of nutritious foods: shin beef instead of fillet steak, for example, or belly pork instead of fillet.

BACON

Look for bags of bacon pieces and meat off-cuts, available in most supermarkets and larger stores.

BATTER

Instead of using water to make a batter, replace it with beer, to add extra flavour.

BISCUITS

To keep biscuits fresh, place a cube of sugar in the tin beside them.

BREAKFAST CEREAL

Make your own breakfast cereal with mixed oats, dried fruit and chopped raw apple.

BREAD

❑ Cut fresh bread into thin slices by dipping the knife into boiling water first.

❏ To get a crispy topping when making your own bread, brush the top with table salt after the second kneading.

BUTTER

To prevent butter burning when using it for frying, add a little cooking oil to the melting butter.

CABBAGE

To keep cabbage fresher longer without needing a refrigerator, try wrapping it in newspaper or standing it in a bowl or bucket of water.

CAKES

❏ Test if a cake is cooked right through by inserting a metal knitting needle into the centre during the cooking process. If the needle comes out clean, the cake is cooked.

❏ A slice of bread in a cake tin will keep the cake moist. Replace stale bread with a fresh piece. For fruit cakes store a fresh eating apple in the tin beside it.

CHEESE

Stop cheese drying out by wrapping it in greaseproof paper and foil or store it in an airtight plastic container in the fridge.

COFFEE

Coffee will retain its flavour longer if stored in the

refrigerator in an airtight container. This applies to fresh and instant coffee.

CONCENTRATES

Use a rolling pin to squeeze out the last remains from tubes containing concentrates, cheese spreads, and so on.

CREAM

If you run out of single cream, substitute the cream with this recipe using 4 parts of milk to 1 part of melted butter.

CUSTARD

Sprinkle sugar on top of hot boiled custard immediately after removing the pan from the heat. This prevents a skin from forming.

EGGS

- ❑ Keep egg yolks fresh in a basin of cold water stored in a cool place.
- ❑ Separate yolk from the white by breaking the egg into a saucer, upturn a small glass over the yolk, and pour off the white.
- ❑ To stop hardboiled eggs discolouring, place them into cold water as soon as the shell has been removed.
- ❑ To stop eggs cracking when boiling, add a small amount of vinegar to the water. Alternatively, prick the air sac within the egg with a sterile sewing needle through the shell, before immersing it in the water.

❑ Stop scrambled egg from sticking to the saucepan by melting a little butter in the pan first and rolling it around the surface.

❑ To check for freshness, remember that old eggs float and fresh eggs sink to the bottom when placed in water.

❑ For a light, fluffy omelette, add a teaspoonful of corn starch to the egg mixture before cooking.

❑ If you accidentally break an egg on the floor, sprinkle salt over it, leave for 10 minutes, and then the egg will be clotted and much easier to pick up.

❑ Your omelettes will be lighter and tastier if you add a dessert-spoonful of water per egg, instead of milk, when beating the eggs.

❑ Don't over do it when beating eggs for omelettes, as too much beating will make them rubbery.

FISH

❑ For a quick sauce, mix some bottled sandwich or cucumber spread with a little bottled salad dressing and a few spoonfuls of milk. Mix to a smooth consistency and heat gently but do not boil.

❑ Make skinning fish easier by dipping your fingers into water and then into salt to give you a better grip on the skin and prevent it from slipping.

❑ Destroy fish smells by rubbing butter into your hands or wherever the smell is coming from.

❑ When shallow frying fish always coat in seasoned flour or egg as it holds the fish together and keeps it moist.

FLOUR

If you run out of self raising flour, it can be replaced with plain flour. All you have to remember is to add 2½ teaspoonfuls of baking powder to every 250g of plain flour.

FRUIT AND VEGETABLES

- Stop peeled apples from discolouring by placing them in cold water to which salt or lemon juice has been added.
- To skin grapes or tomatoes, plunge them into boiling water for a few minutes, then quickly transfer them to cold water.
- To restore fresh taste in frozen vegetables, pour boiling water over them as soon as they come out of the freezer.
- Keep root vegetables fresher longer by removing the tops as soon as you can.
- When baking a fruit pie with sliced or whole fruits, the base often turns out soggy. You can prevent this happening by tossing the fruit in plain flour before spooning it into the pastry basket.

HERBS

- To keep parsley fresh for days, wash it, pat it dry and keep it in an open-ended plastic bag in the fridge. Lettuce can be treated in the same way.
- Keep home-dried herbs fresher longer by keeping them in a screw-topped container stored in a dark place. The same effect can be achieved by keeping the herbs in a dark glass airtight container.

HONEY

Honey is believed to be good for the heart and is said to be blessed with many other health-giving properties.

ICING

Stop icing becoming too brittle by adding a touch of glycerine to the mixture.

LETTUCE

❑ To revive a lettuce, stand it upright in a bowl of water to which a generous amount of vinegar is added.

❑ Revive limp and tired lettuce by standing it for half an hour in a bowl of cold water to which a few drops of lemon juice have been added.

LEMONS

❑ Before squeezing lemons, heat them in boiling water or in a warm oven. This will increase the amount of juice you extract.

❑ Alternatively, putting them in the microwave for half a minute will have the same result.

❑ To prevent apples and pears from oxidising (turning brown) after peeling: squeeze a drop of lemon/lime juice over them. It will keep them pure white for an hour or so.

MEAT AND POULTRY

❑ For a tasty filler for hotpots and stews, try a few suet

dumplings flavoured with herbs. A tasty alternative is to flavour with a few teaspoons of sage and onion stuffing mix.

- ❑ To keep sausages fresh, try boiling them the evening before they are to be eaten. They'll taste better and will not split so easily when fried.
- ❑ Quick porridge oats or fresh breadcrumbs make a good thickening for mince and will increase the bulk. They also make a tasty filler for meatballs and make the meal go further.
- ❑ Try adding a few handfuls of fresh white breadcrumbs to the sausage meat when making Scotch eggs. There'll be little difference to flavour and the meat will go much further.
- ❑ Fresh meat can be sliced very thinly if allowed to freeze until firm before cooking.
- ❑ To slice tinned meat into thin pieces, place the tin in the fridge for an hour or so before opening it.
- ❑ Beef can be tenderised by marinating it in a shallow dish containing white vinegar or pineapple juice. It can be left in this way for several hours. Don't forget to wash away the marinade before cooking, otherwise it will taste of vinegar or pineapple.
- ❑ The taste of cooked turkey or game casserole can be improved by adding a square of bitter chocolate to the casserole.

MILK

Try using reconstituted milk instead of fresh milk in cooked foods where the difference in taste is hard to detect.

MUSHROOMS

Mushrooms keep fresher longer if stored in a paper bag in the salad drawer of the fridge.

OIL

To re-use oil for deep-fat frying, first allow it to cool then strain it through a paper coffee filter.

OVERRIPE BANANAS

Overripe bananas can be mashed and frozen for quick and easy flavouring for cakes and biscuits.

POTATOES

- ❑ Keep peeled new potatoes fresh for days by covering them in water with a few tablespoons of milk added.
- ❑ To make new potatoes easier to scrape, try soaking them for a few minutes in hot water to which a little bicarbonate of soda has been added.
- ❑ To prevent peeled potatoes discolouring overnight, place them in a bowl of water with a slice of fresh bread.
- ❑ Bake potatoes in half the normal time by impaling them on metal skewers. The metal conducts the heat to the centre of the vegetable and saves on cooking time.

RICE

For whiter, fluffier rice try adding a few drops of lemon juice to the water when boiling.

SALT

To stop salt clogging, add some rice to the salt cellar.

SPONGE CAKES

To remove a sponge cake from the tin without it sticking, try standing the tin on a damp cloth for a minute or so before turning out.

SAUCES

When sauces and ketchup refuse to come out of the bottle, try pushing a drinking straw to the bottom. This introduces just enough air to start the flow.

SALTY CASSEROLES

Over-salted casseroles and stews can be remedied by adding a few pieces of raw potato to the mixture.

STALE NUTS

Freshen stale nuts by putting them into the oven at 250 degrees for 15 minutes or so.

TOMATOES

❑ To revive over-ripened tomatoes, try soaking them in cold salted water for up to an hour.

- To ripen green tomatoes place them in a bowl with a ripened tomato or apple.
- Store tomatoes with a few pieces of tissue between them to stop them becoming moist and turning rotten.

WATERCRESS

Keep cut watercress fresher longer by standing it in a basin of water, head first!

WINE

- Don't waste expensive champagne or sparkling wine when it froths upon pulling the cork; dip your finger down the neck of the bottle and the bubbles will subside.
- Providing it hasn't been shaken, properly chilled champagne will not froth out like a fountain. Bubbling over can easily be controlled by covering the cork with a clean teacloth or napkin whilst it is being removed.
- Wine should be poured by holding the bottle by the neck, and lightly supported it with the other hand at the base.
- When pouring wine from a bottle, fill the glasses by holding the bottle at a height of at least 15cm above the glass. This allows the wine to aerate whilst being poured; it will also increase the bouquet of the wine.
- Allow red wines to breathe by pulling the cork an hour before drinking, then serve the wine at room temperature.
- To drink white wines and rosé at their best, they should be de-corked just before serving.

Section 6

Health

ALCOHOL CRAVING

To destroy the desire for alcohol, mix a little goldthread with gold seal in your tea. Ask your health food store to supply the appropriate ingredients.

APPETITE SUPPRESSANT

For an amazing appetite suppressant, before each meal drink one tablespoon of safflower oil mixed with two tablespoons of grapefruit juice.

HEALING FRUITS AND VEGETABLES

All varieties of fruit and vegetables supply your body with important nutrients that keep you fit and well. Many experts advise eating at least 5 items of fruit and vegetables each day. When choosing what to buy, make sure the produce is fresh and plump, and try to eat on the day of purchase.

❏ Beetroot is a great medicine for liver and prostrate.
❏ Papaya is useful for soothing the intestinal tract.
❏ Cherries are a natural remedy for arthritic gout.

- ❏ Pineapple makes a great appetite stimulant.
- ❏ Coconut is good for the stomach.
- ❏ A diet rich in raw apples can ease constipation.
- ❏ Strawberries are high in iron content.
- ❏ Lemons are good for neutralising acid.
- ❏ Watermelon is a natural medicine to benefit the kidneys.
- ❏ Bananas are good for the nerves.
- ❏ Raw apples and grapes are thought to reduce the desire for nicotine.
- ❏ Figs are believed to have cancer-preventing properties.
- ❏ Celery is a natural medicine to benefit the kidneys.
- ❏ Garlic is said to have antibiotic qualities.
- ❏ Oranges are said to be beneficial to the blood.
- ❏ Parsley is a great breath-purifier.
- ❏ Carrots are good for the eyes.
- ❏ Kelp is a rich source of iodine.
- ❏ Green peppers are very rich in Vitamin C.

ICE CURES

- ❏ An ice cube placed on the tongue numbs the tastebuds enough to make taking medicine almost unnoticeable.
- ❏ Similarly, an ice cube placed on the skin makes splinter removal less painful.
- ❏ Stop a burn from blistering by applying ice cubes immediately to the affected area.

INSOMNIA

To help cure insomnia try the following before retiring.

Mix one tablespoon of powdered milk with two tablespoons of honey and add one tablespoon of brewer's yeast. Mix into a paste and stir into a cup of warm milk.

NICOTINE CRAVING

To kill the desire for nicotine, mix half a teaspoon of rochelle salts with a little cream of tartar. This should be taken just before breakfast and will put you off cigarettes for the rest of the day.

TOOTH KNOCKED OUT

A child's tooth can be saved if it is kept warm and moist and is replaced in its socket within 1 or 2 hours. Place the errant tooth in any receptacle with enough milk to cover it. Alternatively, if the child is old enough it can be kept in the child's cheek, or, if you are the parent, in your own cheek, until you can reach a dentist.

Section 7

House Plants And Flowers

Flowering and leafy plants in the home give a great deal of pleasure, but it can be expensive if they are not looked after properly. Follow the rules and you will be well rewarded with brighter blooms for years to come.

❑ When feeding plants with a spray bottle always place plants away from surfaces you do not want to be touched by the spray. A garage or greenhouse is best or else place plants in a large, deep box and spray from above.

❑ Plants should be kept in a cool, even temperature away from draughts and direct heat, including warmth generated by electrical items such as the television set.

❑ Do not place houseplants on top of radiators or other heaters.

❑ Do not leave plants in front of windows, unless curtained or double-glazed.

❑ Protect plants on cold nights by drawing the curtains between them and the window pane.

❑ Prevent greenfly by burying cloves of garlic around all of your plant pots.

❑ During your longer absences, place an old towel in the

bath or sink, saturate with water and stand all of your plants on this to allow slow, gradual watering.

❑ Crumpled chicken wire makes an excellent base for securing flower arrangements for fresh and dried blooms.

❑ Cold used tea bags make a great tonic for plants. Just remove them cold from the pot and place them around the plant and remove when almost dried out.

Section 8

Ironing Tips

Steam irons are an asset for fast and easy ironing. You can control the amount of heat and steam at the touch of a button. But there is more to ironing than just pressing. Read what the experts advise.

- If a garment is too dry to be ironed, pop it into the refrigerator for an hour or so first.
- To unwrinkle a handkerchief, for example if you're on holiday, hand wash it, then smooth it over glass or a mirror and leave it until dry.
- Remove starch marks on an iron by rubbing with a cake of soap while the iron is warm. Remove the surplus with a piece of paper towelling or a clean cloth.
- To remove scorched areas from clothes, wet the affected area with cornstarch and brush off when dry.
- Not everything needs ironing. Underwear and swimwear rarely need ironing and many synthetics actually look better if left hanging to dry naturally and creases are allowed to fall out of their own accord.
- Be careful when pressing hems and seams. And try to iron on the inside of the garment where possible. Ironing

directly onto the seam or hem from the outside will imprint itself and can ruin the garment.

- Try not to wear clothes immediately after ironing. Most things need time to dry after ironing if heavy creasing is to be avoided.
- Iron starched items on the right side. This keeps them clean for longer.
- Turn corduroy articles inside out when ironing, to prevent the wale from becoming flattened.
- Never fill your steam-iron with tap water. Use ionised or distilled water; it will stop your iron becoming clogged with hard water deposits and make it last longer.

Section 9

Jewellery

Most jewellery can be cleaned at home with ordinary household cleaners and brushes. If it's worn a lot, it should be cleaned regularly, say once a month, but if it's seldom worn, then once a year may be enough. When washing your jewellery, do it in a bowl, not over the sink, in lukewarm water, NOT HOT, and when the water is tipped away, run it through a sieve to make sure you are not throwing away the family jewels.

- The most fragile pieces of jewellery are those made of opal, turquoise, pearl, coral, jet, and amber. Wash these pieces of jewellery with a soft toothbrush dipped in a tiny drop of washing up liquid.
- Try cleaning diamonds by dropping them in a tiny amount of whisky or gin.
- To remove scratches from plastic watches, dip a Q-tip in nail polish remover and rub over the face. For deeper scratches dip the Q-tip in clear nail varnish and lightly smooth over the affected area. Rub off surplus immediately.
- Pearls should be worn next to the skin. The oil from the

skin gives them an added lustre, and prevents them from drying out and cracking.

❑ Jade can be washed with any soap, but avoid abrasives as fine scratches will destroy the lustre.

❑ Flawed emeralds should be cleaned with thin greenish coloured oil, because water or other cleaning fluids could make the flaws more visible.

❑ Don't use soap and water to clean antique silver brooches and rings that have stones in them. Sometimes the stones were backed with silver paper, which could become discoloured. Better to have these expensive items cleaned by a professional.

❑ Knotted gold and silver chains can be unknotted by placing them on a sheet of waxed paper and lubricating the chain with thin watch oil. Tease the knots apart using two pins.

Section 10

Financial

MORTGAGE

By paying a little extra off your mortgage every month you can reduce the overall repayment figure by many thousands of pounds. You can also ask your mortgage company to let you repay your loan weekly or fortnightly. This reduces the power of compound interest and means you pay thousands of pounds less in the process.

DEBT

- ❑ Contact the company that you owe the money to and see if they will accept a reduced payment plan to suit your pocket.
- ❑ Don't borrow your way out of debt, you will only end up with bigger debts and a lot of tears.

DISCOUNTS

When shopping, check to see if there is any discount on the goods that you are purchasing, and before paying make sure the discount is still valid. Sometimes, if you don't ask, you don't get.

INSURANCE

Shop around for your home and car insurance. There is a tremendous difference in what companies offer. Over-50s can get cheaper car insurance from most companies. Home contents insurance can be vastly reduced if you fit appropriate locks and alarms to your home.

CREDIT CARDS

Choose a card that doesn't charge an annual fee. When using your card try not to run up a huge debt. The interest rates on credit cards are very high and you could find yourself getting into more and more debt. It would be better to obtain a bank loan at a very favourable interest rate and pay it off at an agreed monthly rate by direct debit.

Section 11

Motoring

RATTLES AND BANGS

Watch for squeaks and unusual noises in your car and have them checked out straight away. These can be the advance warning signs of expensive repair bills just a few miles down the road!

CHOKE CONTROL

If your car has a manual choke, push back the choke as soon as the car is moving and save on fuel costs.

SMOOTH DRIVING

Avoid sudden changes of speed by anticipating traffic lights, school crossing patrols, zebra crossings.

FUEL SAVER

Don't race the engine in neutral and always switch off when caught in lengthy traffic jams and hold-ups.

LOADING

Don't overload the vehicle with passengers or goods. A

heavily laden roof rack can increase fuel consumption considerably.

JERRY CANS

Always carry petrol in a jerry can for emergencies. It's cheaper than calling out a garage if you run out of petrol. Safer too if you travel mostly by night.

AIR FILTERS

A new air filter on your carburettor could save over 3 miles per gallon of fuel.

ENGINE OIL

Make sure the oil level is always topped up on your car. Not doing so could lead to expensive repair bills.

Buy engine oil in bulk for topping up. It's much cheaper than topping up at service stations.

BRAKES

Binding brakes, wrong oil, wrong temperature and tyre pressures all make for uneconomic running. Have them all checked and corrected where necessary.

DEFROSTER

Wipe over your windscreen with a freshly cut potato if there is frost in the air. This is cheaper and just as effective as expensive de-icers. A solution of one part vinegar to three parts water achieves the same objective.

WINDOWS

Disguise chips and dents in windows by plugging with a little colourless nail varnish applied direct from the brush.

TAR REMOVER

Remove tar and paint on your vehicle by cleaning with Benzol.

OIL REMOVER

Remove oil from your driveway by covering the affected area with sand, leave for a few days then brush the area clean.

BATTERIES

Renew a car battery by dissolving 25g of Epsom salts in warm water and adding a little to each cell.

WINDSCREEN CLEANER

After going through the car wash your windscreen will almost always be covered in wax from the soap used in the wash. This can be easily cleaned off by wiping your windscreen over with a damp newspaper. The ink in the newsprint contains spirit which will cut through the wax.

Section 12

In The Garden

AQUARIUM WATER

The water in your aquarium contains many good nutrients that can be put to good use. Next time you change the water, empty it onto your flower borders or into the water butt for later use. Not only will you be saving water but your plants will appreciate every drop.

CUT FLOWERS

❑ When making a display of cut flowers in a vase, don't mix cut daffodils in with the display. Daffodils produce a toxin that kills off the other flowers, so it's better to display them on their own.

❑ Cut roses will keep for 3 to 4 weeks in a vase if you mix 2 tablespoonfuls each of white vinegar and sugar with 1 litre of lukewarm water in your vase.

❑ A few drops of household bleach in the flower vase keeps flowers fresher longer and helps keep the vase stain-free.

VEGETABLE GARDENING

Take a pleasant few minutes to patrol your vegetable

garden at least every other day. This will enable you to harvest produce at its peak of freshness and also scout for pests, disease and other problems. If you catch a problem early, you will have a much better chance of bringing it under control quickly.

FERTILISERS

- ❑ Fresh seaweed, broken up and dug into the garden is many times richer than farmyard manure.
- ❑ Keep egg shells in a warm place until dried thoroughly, then crush finely. This makes an excellent fertiliser for sprinkling around rose bushes.

SEEDLING PROTECTION

Seedlings can be protected by planting in a large, old suitcase. The top can be kept closed in bad weather and lifted in good weather.

CRAZY PAVING

If you need stones for crazy paving, see what your local council can offer. Stones can usually be obtained many times cheaper than from garden centres and other suppliers.

HOMEMADE WATERING CANS

Used washing-up liquid bottles make great watering cans in confined spaces like the greenhouse or lean-to.

BUYING GARDEN TOOLS

Remember that garden tools and other outdoors equipment can be purchased very inexpensively out of season. Most appropriate buying venues include car boot sales, fleamarkets and garage sales.

WEED-FREE PATHS

Salt sprinkled in pavement cracks is an effective weedkiller.

GARDEN HOSES

Make sure there is no water in your garden hose when you store it away in winter. If it freezes the ice can expand and split the hose. Store your hose in a safe place away from extremes of temperature.

COMPOSTING

❑ Make your own compost from grass cuttings and kitchen refuse. This can be kept in a heap in the garden or dug into the soil straight away.
❑ Wet newspaper is a good substitute for compost for planting roses, sweet peas and dahlias.

MARKERS

❑ Ice lolly sticks make good markers.
❑ An old pencil makes an excellent dibber for smaller seedlings.

KNEELING PAD

An old hot water bottle filled with foam or old stockings and tights makes an excellent kneeling pad.

PARSLEY SEEDS

Boiling water poured on parsley seeds before sowing will hasten germination.

PATHS

Reinforce a soggy garden path by tipping used fireplace ashes over it and treading them carefully into the ground.

TOOLS

Remove rust quickly and easily from garden tools with a soap-filled steel-wool pad soaked in paraffin. Finish by rubbing with a piece of crumpled aluminium foil.

POST PRESERVATIVE

To stop new wooden posts from rotting in the ground, cover the base of each with a mixture of raw linseed oil and powdered charcoal before fixing into place.

RUST PREVENTATIVE

Place a few mothballs close to your garden tools to help prevent rusting. Mothballs absorb moisture from the air.

Section 13

Furniture

AGEING FURNITURE

New cupboards and chests look out of place in old houses and country cottages. Now you can make them look like genuine antiques with a varnish and soot treatment. To make the varnish, mix a tin of furniture polish with a little soot added to it, and then use it to polish your furniture.

SCRATCHES

Disguise light scratches on furniture with a wax crayon. Alternatively, rub the scratch with the kernel of a Brazil nut. Machine oil or coloured shoe polish is also very effective for disguising scratches on furniture.

DENTS IN FURNITURE

Small dents in furniture can be steamed out using a steam iron or a damped cloth. Be careful not to overdo it on delicate or very valuable items.

LOOSE DRAWER KNOBS

Old chests of drawers are often provided with large

circular knob-handles. These are apt to pull out with constant wear, and it is not at all uncommon to see a chest with one or more of them missing.

As a rule, knobs are provided with a stem which fits into a hole in the front panel of the drawer; it is held there either by the use of glue or the provision of a screw thread. In both cases there is a likelihood of the hole growing so large that the knob cannot be gripped. When this happens, cut a thin piece of wood about 5cm x 5cm, and fit it on the inside of the drawer over the hole. Then insert the knob from the outside and glue it. Lastly, run a screw from the inside through the piece of wood and into the stem of the knob. It is very unlikely that the knob will ever come off again.

DRAWERS WITH LOOSE BOTTOMS

In the case of cheap furniture the drawers are often made so that in a very short while the bottom falls out. When this happens, examine the drawer. Generally it will be found that a very thin sheet of wood has been used for the bottom and that it has twisted. The bottom should slide into a groove situated at the sides and front of the lower edge of the drawer; but the twisting has pulled it out of position.

To make a good repair, purchase a piece of thin three-ply wood, cut it to the exact size of the bottom, and slide it into the grooves. Before fitting it, run a streak of wood glue along the grooves, and when it is in position, fix a few thin but long panel pins from the outside of the drawer. They need only be inserted along the two sides and not in the front and back.

FREEING STICKY DRAWERS

Rub a candle on the runners of a sticky drawer. It's amazing how much of a difference it will make.

CIGARETTE BURNS ON WOODEN FURNITURE

Make up a paste using equal quantities of white vinegar and baking powder. Rub the burn with the paste using a clean cloth. Finish off by gently rubbing with a pencil eraser to eradicate the mark. If necessary, patch up the mark with some furniture polish or stain.

WHITE RING MARKS

White ring marks on wood, except antiques or valuables, can be removed with a mixture of salt and cooking oil rubbed in gently with a soft cloth.

LEATHER UPHOLSTERY

❑ Leather upholstery can be cleaned and reconditioned simply by smoothing milk into the hide every three months or so. Polish dry with a clean fluff-free duster.

❑ To keep the leather supple and to stop cracking, rub in a good quality leather preservative two to three times a year. Don't use ordinary furniture polish, as it will only make the surface slippery.

PATIO FURNITURE

For cleaning plastic patio furniture, mix 2 tablespoonfuls

washing-up liquid with 4 tablespoonfuls of bleach. Wipe the surfaces with this solution, then leave for 30 minutes. Rinse off with clean water and repeat if necessary. Make sure you protect your hands from the bleach whilst cleaning.

WICKER FURNITURE

- ❑ To keep wicker furniture from turning yellow, wash with a solution of warm salt water.
- ❑ To prevent the wicker from drying out, apply lemon oil every so often.
- ❑ Don't store unused wicker furniture in winter where the temperature can dip below freezing, because the wicker can freeze causing it to split and crack.

CHROME FITTINGS

Clean tarnished chrome with a solution of water and household ammonia. Afterwards, protect the chrome by spraying it with a silicone wax. Pitted chrome fittings can become bright again with chrome cleaner, available from any car accessory shop.

SIMULATED LEATHER UPHOLSTERY

Small spills can be wiped off using a clean damp cloth. But, to be on the safe side, use a good quality simulated leather seat cleaner. Don't use spirit based polishes to get back the shine, as they will only make matters worse.

TEAK FURNITURE

Hardwood such as teak has a very high resin content which should be oiled and not be sealed in the way softwood is dealt with. Linseed oil is excellent for the job and should be applied on a piece of clean cloth and rubbed into the surface.

LIGHT OAK FURNITURE

Light oak furniture can be cleaned with a solution of 1 teaspoonful of household ammonia diluted in 1 litre of water. Apply the solution with a brush then wipe dry with a clean cloth. The surface may be dusted lightly with French chalk afterwards to make the wood lighter.

Section 14

Clothing

ANGORA SWEATERS

After washing and drying your angora sweater, put it in a plastic bag and then leave it in the freezer for an hour or so before putting it away. In this way it will remain nice a fluffy for next time you wear it.

LEATHER CLEANER

You can significantly extend the life and bring back the shine to leather belts and shoes if you first remove small spots of dirt with a damp sponge. Then clean with a silicone fluid.

JEANS

❑ Good quality jeans are expensive and deserve to be looked after. To make them last longer, and look better, turn them inside out the first time you wash them, and don't use any detergent whatsoever.

❑ Break in those stiff jeans and make them soft by washing with detergent and half a cup of table salt.

❑ Some makes of blue jeans have a white line down the crease caused by the fold in the material. This can be got rid of by colouring the line with a mixture of permanent blue ink and water. Dilute the ink until you have the right hue, then brush it on with a soft brush.

ZIP FASTENERS

- ❑ To make a zip fastener run more smoothly, rub the metal teeth with a lead pencil or a little silicone furniture polish.
- ❑ To free a stuck zipper try spraying it with a little shaving foam.

PILLING REMOVER

- ❑ 'Pilling' on shirt collars and knitted garments can be removed with a safety razor.
- ❑ Dust, fluff and 'pilling' on clothing can be removed with a piece of adhesive tape wrapped around your fingers and smoothed carefully across the fabric.

SHINY TROUSERS

- ❑ To remove shine from trousers and skirts, sponge the area with weak ammonia. To make up a solution use one teaspoonful of ammonia to 450ml of water.
- ❑ Alternatively, soak a clean cloth in a solution of one part vinegar to four parts water. Place this over the shiny area and press the garment lightly.

WHITER THAN WHITE SOCKS

To keep socks and lingerie white, try adding a small amount of bicarbonate of soda to the washing water.

LONG-LASTING TIGHTS

Make tights and stockings last longer by putting them in the fridge for an hour or so after washing and drying.

SHOES

- ❏ Patches and scuffs on coloured shoes can be camouflaged with children's gloss paints.
- ❏ Remove saltwater marks with a mixture of white vinegar and water in equal parts.
- ❏ To dry out wet shoes and boots pack them with screwed-up paper.
- ❏ Apply stick-on soles to new shoes to save on expensive repair bills later.
- ❏ Buy new shoes in the morning before you start doing other shopping. Your feet will be cool and fresh, and they will not be swollen with the heat of being on your feet all day.

Section 15

Sewing And Knitting

SOFT TOYS

For stuffing soft toys, try using old tights and stockings or shredded and unravelled knitted garments.

THREADING NEEDLES

To make threading a needle easier, hold the needle against something white, like a piece of paper, or try holding it up to a light surface like a white wall or the sky.

BUTTONS

- Remove buttons before discarding clothing.
- Make buttons stay longer on the garment by painting the thread with colourless nail polish, particularly on children's clothing.

KNITTING

Knitters will find that balls of yarn kept in a nylon stocking during use will keep them from tangling, and will make them flow more smoothly. The same thing can be accomplished by keeping each ball of wool in a small jam jar with a hole in the lid through which the yarn can be drawn.

SEWING

When working with slippery material, try sticking a piece of waxed paper along the seams and pull away when finished. The same thing can be accomplished with adhesive tape applied along the edges you are working on and removed once the stitches are in place.

COLLARS

It's usual for the shirt collar to wear out and the rest of the shirt to look like new. With a bit of needlework the collar can be removed and turned, making the shirt last twice as long.

Section 16

Pets

MOVING TO A NEW HOME

Moving is a traumatic experience for everyone, most of all family pets. The movement, confusion and disruption can easily bewilder your pet and lead him to run off and hide, even before the removal van appears. To prevent this, keep your cat indoors as near to removal day as possible.

Keep him somewhere quiet in a room which has already been cleared and with close access to a litter tray, food and drink. Let him travel with you if possible or in a secure pet carrier if appropriate. When you arrive at your new home, keep him confined to one room with familiar furniture and belongings.

Make sure he has his own toys, bedding and feeding utensils close by. Keep him indoors for several days with a litter tray close by, gradually introducing him to more rooms and eventually allowing him into the garden under close supervision. Bring him indoors and feed him a favourite meal and make a fuss of him.

Do this for a few days before allowing him out alone. By this time he will be acclimatised to his new surroundings and know that a good meal and a warm welcome await him at home.

BREEDING CATS

Apart from your queen, you'll need a suitable stud, either your own or someone else's. You'll also need an understanding of health care, especially during pregnancy and birth and you must be prepared to provide extra food and attention for your cat from pregnancy onwards. You must be able (and willing) to pay for appropriate veterinary care if needed and you should check out potential buyers or owners for your kittens before your cat is mated.

CAT SCRATCH-POST

To stop your cat from scratching the furniture, give it a scratch-post so that it can sharpen its claws whenever it likes. To make a scratch-post, you will need a wooden base made from a piece of block-board, 30cm x 30cm; a post made from an old broom handle about 60cm long; and some carpet remnants. Make a hole in the centre of the base large enough to fit the broom handle. Fix the two together so that they won't come apart, then staple the carpet around the post. Spray some catnip on the scratch-post now and then. You can also hang small cat toys to the post to keep your cat amused.

RESTRAINING PETS

Keep dogs and cats at bay by placing moth balls in areas you want them to avoid.

PET APPETISER

When your pet has no appetite try offering him a saucer of beer. It makes a great appetiser.

PET SHAMPOO

For a great dry shampoo for your pet, rub baking soda into the fur and brush out immediately afterwards.

HEALTH CHECKS

- ❑ Check your pets regularly in summer for wounds or grazes which can fester easily in the warmer weather.
- ❑ Check your pet's eyes, ears and feet for grass seeds which can eventually embed themselves in skin and other delicate areas with very painful consequences.

WARM WEATHER

- ❑ Don't leave your pet in the car in warm weather with the windows closed. And always have a spare key available in case of emergencies.
- ❑ Don't leave pet birds in conservatories during the warmer months where they can dehydrate very quickly and possibly die.

GROOMING

You can use the suction tool of your vacuum cleaner to groom your dog.

PUPPIES

- ❏ Try putting a ticking clock somewhere close to your new puppy's bed. The sound should console him until he settles into his new home.
- ❏ Keep new and very young puppies in a children's playpen when you have to leave them unattended for any length of time.

FISH

Only feed fish the amount they can eat in five minutes. Overfeeding is a common cause of death in tropical fish and goldfish.

- ❏ Do not touch fish with your dry hands. This causes damage to their delicate skins. Always scoop fish out with a special net or transfer them direct from one source of water to another.

SONG BIRDS

To encourage your budgie or canary to sing, tape his own song and play it back to him. To teach him to talk, play a recording of your voice with messages you'd like him to repeat.

HAMSTERS

A jam jar on its side makes a good toilet for a hamster. Keep it in one corner of the cage where the animal will get used to it and this will keep the rest of the cage clean for longer periods.

Section 17

Pests

ANT DETERRENT

- When ants decide to move in with you it would be foolhardy to use an ant killer product in the house, especially in the kitchen. Try to find the point of entry and stuff-up the hole with a cotton-wool bud soaked in essence of peppermint. Ants don't like peppermint so will look for another suitable place to socialise.
- If you do need to kill off an ants' nest sprinkle a mixture of sugar and borax near the nest.

MICE

- If you have mice, think about getting a cat rather than using mousetraps or poison, neither of which are suitable in the normal family environment, especially where there are children.
- To catch elusive mice in the home without killing them, place a humane mouse trap (that's a trap with a fast action door closer) on their run, close to the skirting board. Leave a little peanut butter, bacon, and/or nuts in the trap, as these foods seem to be most attractive. Empty

the trap at least a mile away from home, preferably in a field away from other people's homes.

SILVERFISH

- If you are troubled with silverfish try placing whole cloves in the wardrobes and drawers.
- Eliminate silverfish by sprinkling Epsom salts at the back of cupboards and drawers. Make sure the Epsom salts don't come into contact with the contents of the cupboard or drawer.
- To get rid of silverfish, sprinkle a little sugar and borax mix (equal parts). Do not do this where there are children in the house.

FLEA ERADICATOR

- Getting rid of fleas in a pet's bed need no longer be troublesome. Purchase a new flea collar, cut it into four pieces and place under your pet's bed or cushion. If you renew the collar when the flea repellent wears off it will keep the fleas away for good.
- Another tip: to rid your pet of fleas include a foam rubber pad in his bedding. Fleas positively hate it.
- After vacuuming carpet and rugs, store the vacuum cleaner in the garage. If it is kept in a cupboard inside the house, the fleas will jump out of the vacuum cleaner and return.

GARDEN SLUGS

Trap slugs by placing half an inverted grapefruit skin on the soil's surface with a few slug pellets underneath. Alternatively, put a small tin in the ground, level with the soil, and half-filled with water mixed with milk. Slugs will be attracted to the mixture and will drown.

WASPS

Wasps can be got rid of by lining your window sills with jars filled with a mixture of honey, detergent and water. The wasps will be drawn to the mixture and drown.

EARWIGS

Barrier insecticides, such as 'Vapona Insectipen', can help keep earwigs out of the kitchen.

WOODLICE

For woodlice, place a peeled baked potato in a flower pot close to where the main problem is. This will encourage the woodlice into the pot which can be moved to a more suitable location.

Section 18

Appliance Repair

Don't be a bright spark when working with live electrical equipment. Follow the first rule of safety and switch off and unplug the appliance before you reach for the screwdriver. Take care not to lose the screws and bolts when opening a piece of equipment; place them in the sequence that you removed them on a strip of blue-tack, and replace them in the reverse sequence.

CAR RADIO AERIAL

A wire coat hanger works well as a temporary measure for a broken car radio aerial. Pull the coat hanger into a diamond shape, straighten the hook, and place the end of the hook in the central hole of the aerial socket.

CAMCORDERS

❑ When carrying your camcorder on the beach or in a small boat, protect it by keeping it in its holder and then placing the holder in a plastic bag.

❑ If it starts to rain while you're filming and your camcorder gets wet, wipe the surfaces with a soft cloth, then remove the battery and don't use the camcorder again until it is perfectly dry.

ELECTRIC GRASS MOWERS

When mowing the lawn special care must be taken to make sure that the electric cables run behind the lawnmower. Never allow the cable to get in front of the mower, the slightest distraction can cause a fatal accident. You should always us an RCD device, which will cut the power should the cable get damaged. Never use an electric mower in wet conditions, because apart from damaging the motor, you can end up electrocuting yourself.

ELECTRIC PLUGS

Never overload a socket with too many plugs or adapters, and make sure they are correctly fused.

GAS HOBS

□ Sometimes the gas flame from the jets on a gas hob is uneven due to some of the jets getting clogged up with burnt-on food overspills. Prevent this problem with regular cleaning in hot soapy water, using a spent matchstick for cleaning the holes.

□ To remove particularly tough burnt-on stains, clean with acetone on a rag. Be sure to allow adequate ventilation when using acetone as the fumes can be hazardous.

LIGHT BULBS

- You'll get a better light for longer if you clean light bulbs regularly with a feather duster.
- Fly marks on bulbs can be removed with a drop of white vinegar on a piece of clean soft cloth. Make sure the bulb is dry before you switch on the power.
- To remove a broken light bulb safely, take a piece of soap and press the soggy end gently over the jagged edges of the light bulb. When firmly in place, use the soap as a handle to remove the bulb.

MICROWAVE OVENS

- Always unplug your microwave oven from the mains when cleaning.
- Your microwave oven will be more efficient, and last longer if you clean it regularly with a cloth wrung out in a bowl of hot soapy water to which a few soda crystals have been added.
- Abrasives and wire wool can seriously damage the coated surfaces of your microwave. Spray cleaners should never be used because the spray can enter the various holes in the panels behind which are electrical parts.
- If the inside panels have become spattered with fat and stubborn burn-on food, wipe-off as much as possible, then steam off the remainder by heating a small shallow dish of water at the highest microwave level. Then clean in the normal way; this method will also dispel nasty lingering odours.

TOASTERS

If you accidentally allow a plastic wrapper to come into contact with your toaster, it will probably melt hard onto the side. Disconnect the toaster and use nail varnish remover to clean it off.

VACUUM CLEANERS

If you are getting poor suction with your vacuum cleaner, it is probably due to the hose being blocked. Look in the hose to see if there is an obstruction, and if there is use something like a bamboo cane to unblock it.

VIDEO RECORDERS

When the picture quality begins to fade and the sound gets fuzzy it's time to clean the tape-heads. Use a head-cleaning tape to solve this problem. They are available at all good retail music shops.

WASHING MACHINES

If your washing machine is making noisy vibrations and trying to move across the floor, then it is probably standing unevenly. Check to see if the two front adjustable feet are both touching the floor. If wrongly adjusted you may need the help of a second person to raise the machine slightly whilst you adjust the feet. Finally, use a spirit level to check that the machine is standing evenly.

Section 19

Beauty

MOUTHWASH

Instead of buying expensive mouthwashes, try gargling with salt dissolved in water.

POWDER PUFF

Cotton wool balls make an excellent substitute for powder puffs.

FACE POWDER

- ❑ Talc can be used instead of face powder, but beware of using too much.
- ❑ A small amount of talc mixed with your face powder will make it last longer and will make very little difference to the colour. Baby talc is particularly useful.

SKIN TONIC

Make your own skin tonic from 25ml of liquid honey mixed with 225ml of witch hazel or rose water.

LIPSTICK

Use a lip-brush to get at the very last of your lipstick.

COTTON WOOL

Ordinary cotton wool can be doubled in size by placing it in a warm airing cupboard or on a radiator for an hour or two.

HAIR

- For dry hair, try rubbing castor oil into the roots before shampooing.
- Plastic cocktail sticks make excellent roller pins when putting your hair up in curlers.
- To help clear dandruff, before shampooing rinse your hair with a cupful of equal parts of vinegar and water.
- To add shine to their hair, brunettes should use a solution of equal parts of vinegar and water to the final rinse, while blondes will find a little lemon juice accomplishes much the same thing.

NAILS STRENGTHENED

- To strengthen nails, soak the fingertips in a cup of warm water to which a tablespoon of bicarbonate of soda has been added.
- Soak the fingertips in a little warm olive oil to soften the cuticles prior to a manicure.

NAIL POLISH

To stop a nail polish bottle cap sticking, grease the grooves and ridges with petroleum jelly.

SUNBURN COOLANT

Soothe sunburn by massaging with milk to which a pinch of bicarbonate of soda has been added.

TIRED EYES

Use pads of cotton wool soaked in witch hazel as a tonic for tired eyes. Just lie down for ten minutes with a damp compress over each eye. Slices of cucumber or fresh potato are also effective.

TIRED SKIN

To wake up tired skin, try making an oatmeal face pack. Two tablespoons of oatmeal are needed to three tablespoons of milk. Add a teaspoon of rosewater and smooth into a paste. This should be spread over the face and neck and left for about fifteen minutes before rinsing thoroughly.

Section 20

Children

BATHTIME WITHOUT TEARS

When washing children's hair at bathtime, keep shampoo out of their eyes by smearing a line of petroleum jelly across the forehead and down both sides of the face.

ELECTRIC SOCKETS

Protect children from electrical sockets by sealing off the holes with adhesive tape or electrical tape when not in use.

GLASS DOORS

Protect very young children from glass doors by smoothing clear contact paper over the glass. When they're a bit older, a few stickers or net curtains can be used to deter them from walking into the glass.

COLOURED PAPER DANGER

Do not burn coloured newspaper or magazines in your fireplace! They contain lead and when burned will emit dangerous levels of the lead. This can be extremely harmful especially to children!

GOLD FISH PONDS

Protect very young children from falling into the water by covering the pond with strong wire netting.

KITCHEN CUPBOARDS

The kitchen is always a very interesting place for youngsters. Unfortunately, it can also be a place of danger. Lock away or put out of reach all your cleaning materials, so that little hands cannot get hold of them. Cupboards that haven't got locks can be secured with nylon ties that can only be undone by a grown-up.

Section 21

D.I.Y.

NAILS

- ❑ Prevent nails from splitting wood by blunting the nail slightly first. Alternatively, stick a piece of adhesive tape over the area before hammering in the nail.
- ❑ Try not to run a line of nails along the same wood grain, otherwise the wood could split.
- ❑ Or, to stop nails from splitting wood drill a small guide hole beforehand.

PLASTIC BAG HOLDER

Don't throw away plastic bags that have only been used once. Save them in an empty tissue box for reuse when you need a bag in a hurry.

DRILLING GLASS AND CERAMICS

- ❑ To help judge how deep you are drilling, place the screw against the drill bit and mark the length on the bit with a pen or crayon, or use a bit of masking tape.
- ❑ When drilling ceramic tiles or other glazed surfaces, stick a piece of adhesive tape on the surface and mark where

the hole is to be drilled. In this way the drill will not slip over the glazed surface. By the way, never use a hammer action drill.

❏ When drilling masonry, always withdraw the tip every 5 seconds or so to stop it overheating. If you don't keep the tip cool it damages the drill.

SANDPAPER PRESERVER

Make sandpaper last longer by backing it with masking tape.

PAINTING

❏ For drip-free painting, punch several dents around the rim of a bucket to remove excess paint from the brush.

❏ To take the lumps out of paint, cut a piece of screen (heavy lino is great) to fit inside the can or bucket. This will sink to the bottom and take the lumps with it.

❏ Stop skin forming on top of paint left in an open tin by pouring a little turpentine onto the surface of the paint. Pour off the turpentine when you resume painting.

RAWLPLUGS

Spent matches make a great emergency substitute for rawlplugs.

LIGHTING

❏ There's nothing worse than a dingy, dimly-lit room to make you feel miserable. To brighten your life, go to your

local DIY superstore and buy a pot of emulsion paint. Your wall will look great in a beautiful autumnal shade, and the wall will reflect the light better.
❑ While you're in the decorating mood, why not change your lampshades to a white or light-pastel shade to help them emit more light?

LUBRICANT

A drop of glycerine makes an excellent lubricant for household appliances and other objects with moving metal parts.

SCREWS

❑ Remove a stubborn screw by heating it first with a soldering iron. Then with your screwdriver in place, give it a sharp jerk in a clockwise direction before abruptly changing direction to anti-clockwise.
❑ A drop or two of vinegar or oil can help shift rusty screws.

POLYSTYRENE CUTTER

Cut polystyrene tiles without cracking by cutting with a knife heated in boiling water.

RUBBER GLOVES

To get more mileage out of rubber gloves, turn them inside out when new and stick a strip of sticking plaster across the top of each finger. This is especially useful for preventing damage by anyone with long or pointed fingernails.

HOT WATER BOTTLES

Hot water bottles will last longer if they are completely dried out when the cold weather ends. Simply hang them upside down for a day or so and afterwards put a little French chalk inside them before blowing them up slightly and inserting the stopper. The air keeps the sides apart and prevents the rubber sticking.

NEW DUSTERS

Keep old candlewick bedcovers for cutting up and using as dusters and polishing cloths.

BATTERIES

Do not use new batteries alongside old ones. The new ones try to recharge the old and lose some of their own power. And always remove batteries from appliances which are likely to go unused for long periods of time.

SCISSORS SHARPENER

Use kitchen aluminium foil to sharpen your scissors. Fold a small piece of aluminium foil in half, and then in half again, then cut it into narrow strips. Alternatively, you can do the same thing with a sheet of medium-grade sand paper.

LADDER SAFETY

☐ Before climbing a ladder, make sure that the foot of the ladder is placed a safe distance from the wall in comparison with the height of the ladder. For example, if the ladder is 4 metres high, then the base of the ladder should be 1 metre from the wall.

☐ Ladders should be placed on a firm level surface, and the top should be resting on something solid, and not on guttering or a windowsill.

☐ Always chock the base of the ladder to stop it slipping. Better still, ask someone to hold it for you.

SCAFFOLDING

Scaffolding towers must be erected on firm ground. If the tower is more than 3.25 metres high for a 1.3 metre square base it must be tied to the building.

NAILS IN CRUMBLING PLASTER

Sometimes it is necessary to drive a nail in a wall but the plaster is so crumbly that the nail will not hold. An excellent idea is to make the hole for the nail first, and then to fill the opening with plaster filler. This done, the nail is pushed into the filler and left until the filler hardens. When hardened, it will be strong enough to support almost any weight.

DAMP CUPBOARDS

It is quite usual for damp and mildew to form in cupboards attached to the inner surface of outside walls in old houses. An extremely useful remedy is to paint the damp patches with waterproofing paint. When dry make a frame with 50mm x 25mm battening to cover the wall in the back of the cupboard. Fit 50mm thick fibreglass insulation inside the frame, keeping it in place with a sheet of plastic. Then affix a sheet of plasterboard over the battening and insulation, nailing it in place to the battening. Finally, decorate to the desired colour. Your cupboard will never get damp again.

This same method can be adapted to the inside of outside walls where considerably cold surfaces are experienced due to the walls not being insulated.

Section 22

Travelling

- ❑ Travel when fares are cheapest. Some travel companies, including bus and rail, allow senior citizens and children to travel at reduced rates on certain days or on specific routes.
- ❑ Walk to keep fit and save on bus fares.
- ❑ If you travel regularly by rail and tube or on certain bus routes, consider buying a season ticket.
- ❑ Where possible, obtain a combined tube and bus season ticket.
- ❑ If you can travel any day you like, think about weekend specials on trains and buses.
- ❑ Ask rail and bus companies about 'book ahead' specials where savings can be significant.
- ❑ Organise trips to do as many errands as possible in a single journey.
- ❑ Scan your travel document details then email them to yourself. You can then retrieve them if they get lost or stolen. Do the same with the relevant pages on your passport.
- ❑ Don't use the locks that came in your suitcases, as a

fingernail file can open them. Buy your own small padlocks and use them instead.

❑ If you normally get an upset stomach while travelling, carry pieces of ginger with you in a plastic food bag. Chew on them and your stomach will soon be better.

❑ Avoid flying if you have cold, flu or hay fever. If you have to fly take an oral decongestant before and after landing.

❑ To prevent ear popping when travelling by air, suck sweets, sip drinks, swallow, chew or yawn when problems start to occur. Let babies suck a bottle or dummy to help them avoid earache.

Section 23

Shopping

- Shop just once a week to cut down on expensive impulse buying.
- Plan your menus in advance and stick to your shopping list.
- Don't shop when you are hungry. Research reveals that hungry shoppers buy more and of all the wrong things.
- Resist the urge to touch or pick up an item unless you really want it. Researchers say, if you touch it, you're many times more likely to buy it.
- Think big. You can always save money by buying larger, economy packets.
- When buying fruit and vegetables at a market stall, make sure you see what the stall-holder wraps for you. It could be your turn to get all the specks.
- At the checkout make sure the assistants properly process special offers in your trolley.
- Stock up with non-perishable items you use regularly whenever they are on special offer in supermarkets and discount stores.
- When buying single, one-price oranges and grapefruit,

pick them out by weight, not by size. A large one that feels light will have thick skin. A heavy one will contain more fruit and juice.

- Weigh everything when you get home and return anything which is short-weight.
- Vary your shopping according to the time of year. Fruit, vegetables and meat all have seasons when they are at their best, and cheapest. Think about stocking up your freezer with in-season products.
- Make shopping less convenient by leaving your credit cards at home. Better still, cancel your credit cards and shop with cash only.
- Think twice before making any major purchase. Shop around to see what savings are possible. View a copy of *Which?* magazine in your local library to discover what their researchers have to say about the product you are contemplating.
- Form a buying group. Buy in bulk, where high savings are possible, and distribute items between members.
- Don't be afraid to ask for discounts when paying cash for major items like television sets, dishwashers and carpets.
- Look for 'own brands' in the shops. This way you won't pay over the odds for fancy packaging.
- Check the thrift and discount stores in your area for really good discounts.
- For household bargains, check your local newspaper and look in shop windows for second-hand bargains.

- ❑ Pay off credit card charges at the appropriate time each month to save on interest charges.
- ❑ Collect whatever food and grocery coupons you see in magazines and newspapers. File these in date order and always check this month's expiry dates before shopping.
- ❑ Some things are cheaper in a warehouse club, but not all. Check your prices.
- ❑ Don't be brand loyal. Be willing to switch brands.
- ❑ Honour your spending limit.
- ❑ Don't buy it if you won't use it – even if it is in the sale.

Section 24

Safety

❏ Store sharp knives in a drawer or knife rack and always lock them away when young children are around.

❏ Have fire guards securely fixed to the wall or fireplace when young children and elderly people are around.

❏ Do not take hairdryers or other electrical appliances into the bathroom and never use these appliances when your hands are wet.

❏ Store bleaches and cleaning agents out of reach of young children.

❏ Never use solvents, paints or adhesives in the same room as naked flames. This applies to lighter fuel which is a major cause of house fires.

❏ Never mix toilet cleaner with other cleaning materials. This can cause toxic fumes.

❏ Close all doors before retiring for the night. This simple practice can save lives in the event of a fire.

❏ Have chimneys cleaned regularly.

❏ Have a fire escape plan and practice it regularly. Make sure all family members know where spare keys are kept.

❏ Do not use aerosols near naked flames or leave spray cans

close to a heat source. These can explode and cause serious injury.

❑ Never leave a chip pan unattended and always keep a wrung-out tea towel close by to throw over the pan in the event of a fire.

❑ Never, ever throw water over a chip pan fire.

❑ Dry chips with paper kitchen towel before submerging them in boiling oil or fat.

Section 25

Security

- ❑ Never leave valuables in view of passers by, especially out of doors. Keep all valuables hidden on your person or tucked away out of view in the car or in baggage you will be taking with you.
- ❑ Mark valuables like bikes and cars with your name and address or just the postcode.
- ❑ Photograph valuable antiques and jewellery. Write details on the reverse of the photographs and keep these in a separate place to the items themselves, such as in a bank vault or a friend's house.
- ❑ A baby alarm can alert you to intruders downstairs. Keep one switched on downstairs while you sleep upstairs.
- ❑ Lock away ladders and tools which might be used to break into your home or cause damage to your possessions. Always make sure your car is locked at night and the key kept out of sight.
- ❑ If ladders and toolkits must be kept out of doors, at least chain and padlock them securely.
- ❑ Check your insurance policy to see whether safety and security precautions you've taken entitle you to discount.

❑ Always cancel newspapers and milk in person before you set off on holiday. Don't leave it to someone else and remember that notes and verbal messages to others can be inadvertently broadcast to 'undesirables'.

❑ Never put your home address on luggage labels. Always use your work address or flight number.

❑ If you leave your car in a long stay car park, take care not to leave anything with your name and address on it.